Contents

1 What's in a name?

One of the most obvious links we have with our past is our surnames. My surname tells me that one of my ancestors, many centuries ago, was a blacksmith. Does your surname suggest the trade of one of your forefathers? If not, it may tell you the name of one of your ancestors. Names such as Robinson, Mac Dermott or Fitzgerald tell us that many generations ago a man was given a name meaning 'son of' Robin or Dermot or Gerald. As well as this kind of information, can surnames tell us anything about the Normans in Ireland?

Typically Irish?

Many people would consider the surnames listed below to be typically Irish. In fact they were brought here by the Normans who invaded and colonised Ireland at the end of the twelfth century.

1 *Some important people in history, politics, sport and entertainment have surnames in the list. Can you think of any?*

2 *Some of these names, like Bermingham, carry a clue as to where their families came from before they arrived in Ireland. Which can you identify?*

3 *The names 'Conor Cruise O Brien' and 'John Fitzgerald Kennedy' have something in common. What is it?*

4 *Do people in Ireland today usually distinguish between Norman surnames and Irish surnames, such as O Connor, Mac Carthy, O Brien or Kennedy?*

Barnwell	Dillon	Purcell
Barrett	Dowdall	Roche
Barry	Fitzgerald	Russell
Bermingham	Fitzmaurice	Sarsfield
Bruton	Fleming	Savage
Burke	Gaffney	Sinnot
Butler	Grace	Stafford
Clinton	Keating	Stapleton
Cody	Lacy	Staunton
Condon	Lockhart	Taaf/Taaffe
Coogan	Logan	Talbot
Corish	Lynnot	Tobin
Costello	Nangle	Tracy
Cruise	Nugent	Tuite
Cusack	Peppard	Walsh/Welsh
Dalton	Plunket	White
Delany	Power	Wogan

Very few of the people we call Normans actually came to Ireland from Normandy. Historians also call them 'Anglo-Normans' because most came from England or Wales. Their ancestors had conquered England a hundred years earlier. By the time they came to Ireland they were just beginning to call themselves 'English', but they still spoke French and were proud of their Norman roots. As time went by these Anglo-Normans in Ireland saw themselves as different from the English living in England and so they are often called 'Anglo-Irish'. Words are signposts. All these signs, whatever their spelling, point towards the invaders who arrived in Ireland in 1169.

A Family names in Ireland today

5 *Take a piece of paper and move it down the map so that you can find the names on page 4. How many appear in each of these groups of counties?*

Donegal - Derry - Tyrone;

Antrim - Down - Armagh;

Dublin - Meath - Kildare;

Waterford - Cork - Kerry - Wexford

6 *Do the numbers tell you anything about where the largest numbers of Normans settled?*

(From *Encyclopaedia of Ireland*, 1968)

Lenny Murphy was the leader of a gang called 'the Shankill Butchers' which murdered many Catholics in Belfast in the 1970s. Murphy has been described as 'a young man warped by bitter hatred of Catholics caused partly by ragging when he was a child because of his "Catholic surname"' (Irish Times, 3 August, 1989). Does the idea of a 'Catholic' or 'Protestant' surname make any sense?

2 Did the Normans leave any traces?

A historian wrote that 'the Norman invasion was the most far-reaching event that occurred in Ireland since the introduction of Christianity'. How could we test his statement? We could pin-point the things which the Normans left to the people who came after them. Things which are left behind for others are called a 'legacy'. They are what we inherit, part of our heritage. What was the Norman legacy? Secondly, we could ask what Ireland was like before the Normans came and then identify what impact they had on the Irish way of life.

The Norman legacy

1 Before the Normans came:
   a) Which language did people speak throughout Ireland?
   b) What system of law did they use?

2 In which barony do you live?

3 Today Ireland is a 'parliamentary democracy'. What does this mean?

4 Which part of the island is still linked to the United Kingdom?

This book is written in English, which is the first spoken language of most people in Ireland today. English was first written and spoken in Ireland by the Normans. The Normans and their descendants started to replace the ancient system of Irish law with the English system of Common Law on which our laws are based today. The Normans were the first to hold parliaments in Ireland and it was they who first brought the island under the control of the English Crown.

Our speech, our system of government, our political divisions; we take all these things for granted and all can be seen to be the legacy of the Normans. But these parts of their legacy are mostly 'invisible'. The Normans also left very 'visible' traces. You can still see the remains of over 2,000 castles built by the Normans. They founded many important towns such as Coleraine, Carrickfergus, Dundalk, Drogheda, Kilkenny, Tralee, Galway, Sligo and Clonmel. The Normans left us a varied and important legacy.

What was Ireland like before the Normans?

When the first Normans arrived in 1169 they thought the country was much less well developed than England, South Wales and France, where they had lived before. The few important towns such as Dublin and Waterford had been founded by the Vikings. The descendants of these Vikings still lived in these towns in the 1160s. The Irish preferred to live in smaller groups in the countryside. The archaeologists who have dug up the remains of their homes and farms call them 'dispersed settlements' because each group of farmers was separate from the others.

These settlements were so spread out that there was little trade between them and no need for coins. Goods were bought and sold by exchanging cattle. This was quite natural because Irish farmers preferred to raise cattle than plant crops and vegetables in the field – most still do! The Normans, who lived on wine and bread, looked down on the Irish who lived on milk and meat.

The pattern of families was different too. The Irish thought of themselves as belonging to a large group made up of their close and distant relatives. Today we call this a 'kin-group'. The Normans thought of only their close relatives as their family.

In England, by the middle of the twelfth century, one king ruled the whole country and this had been the case for about two hundred years. Gradually, Ireland was also moving towards having only one king, the high-king. Two hundred years earlier there had been many small kingdoms but when the Normans started to arrive these had merged into a smaller number of powerful kingdoms with one high-king, Rory O Connor, who claimed to be above them all.

A The most important Irish kingdoms in 1169

5 Which names on the map are still used today?

6 Which are no longer generally used?

1 Which is the nearest castle to your school or home? Who built it? In which century was it first built?

2 We have come across the word 'legacy' several times when talking about the Normans. What do we mean by this word? Has it any other meaning?

3 Ireland and Europe: Have things changed?

The Normans originally came from Normandy in northern France. When they arrived in Ireland in 1169 they had already conquered Sicily, England and much of Wales. There had been contacts between Ireland and Europe before the Normans, but after 1169 there was a political link through the Norman kings and barons. Just over 800 years later, in 1973, Ireland and Northern Ireland (with the United Kingdom) joined the European Economic Community. Are there any ways in which Ireland's position in Europe was the same in the twelfth century as it is today?

In the Middle Ages Europeans believed that the Mediterranean Sea was the centre of the world. 'Mediterranean' means 'middle of the earth'. To Europeans Ireland was on the edge of the world. In Unit 2 we saw that those who visited Ireland saw it as being very different from France or England. The Irish knew that many of their customs were unlike those of other countries, but they were not ashamed of this. Indeed, they believed their own ways to be superior. In the middle of the twelfth century St Malachy, an Irishman who had lived in France, tried to build a church in the French fashion at Bangor in County Down but the local people objected, saying 'Why have you thought good to introduce this novelty into our regions? We are Irish, not French'.

On the edge

A1 *A fifteenth-century map of Europe*

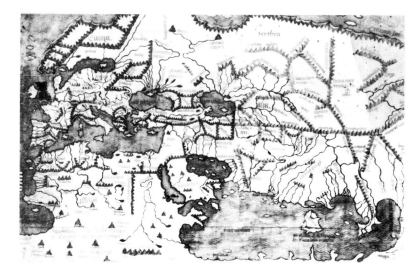

1 *When did the Normans conquer England?*

2 *How accurately is Ireland drawn on the map compared with Italy? What do you learn from the difference?*

3 *There are two Lough Dergs. Which did the pilgrim visit? Why did he go there?*

A2 "All we Irish, inhabitants of the world's edge, are disciples of Saints Peter and Paul."

(St Columbanus, sixth century)

A3 "I arrived at the end of the world in Ireland, which is the most remote province of the western world."

(Spanish pilgrim travelling to Lough Derg, in the fourteenth century)

Still on the edge?

The European Community is divided into central areas which have well-developed industries and the areas on the edge or periphery which have much less well-developed industries.

B The European Community in 1988

4 *What is the difference between Northern Ireland and the Republic on the map? What reasons would you give for the difference?*

5 *What other regions are considered 'outer peripheral' like Ireland? What have they all in common?*

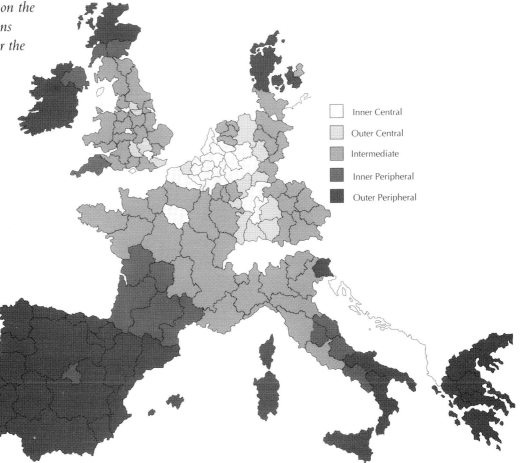

Inner Central
Outer Central
Intermediate
Inner Peripheral
Outer Peripheral

C A view of Ireland and Europe in 1990

6 *Are there ways in which the bishop and St Malachy hold similar ideas? What are they?*

"Ireland continues to be too inward-looking, too parochial in its vision and should become more 'Euro-conscious' as a new Europe is formed before our eyes."

(Bishop of Down and Connor, *Irish Times*, 7 September, 1990)

1 *Should it surprise us that European fashions reach Ireland late and are given an Irish flavour when they arrive? Why?*

2 *What examples would you give of things changing more slowly in Ireland than in the rest of Europe?*

3 *What are the advantages and disadvantages of living 'on the edge' of Europe?*

4 Why did the Normans come?

We could easily find out *when* the Normans came to Ireland, *where* they landed and *how* they travelled, but that would not satisfy our curiosity. We are more interested in *why* they came here in the first place. Let us see if we can find the answer to this question in Ireland.

Winners and losers

In Unit 2 you read that Rory O Connor, king of Connacht, was high-king when the Normans came. No man became high-king simply because other kings all agreed. There was usually fighting to prove who had the strongest support. Rory's first step to becoming high-king was to organise a rebellion in Ailech against its king (see map, Unit 2). The king was killed so the men of Ailech had no choice but to follow Rory. He then got the support of Tiernan O Rourke, king of Breifne. Breifne was a small kingdom between Connacht and Ailech and was weaker than they were. However, having Tiernan on his side gave Rory a strong say in what Meath did because Tiernan's wife came from the family which ruled Meath.

So wars and marriage gave Rory the support of all the kingdoms in the north and midlands and he became high-king. But this was not to the liking of Dermot Mac Murrough, king of Leinster. He had wanted to be high-king. In 1152 he had even taken Tiernan O Rourke's wife from her husband, hoping that way to get Meath on his side. All he managed to do was to make Tiernan a bitter enemy. After Rory became high-king even Dermot's own men in Leinster deserted him. Dermot needed new supporters and warriors. He already had links through trade with Wales and south-west England and so in August 1166 he set sail for England to look for foreign help.

Dermot Mac Murrough – villain or hero?

Irish writers call him 'Diarmait na nGall' or 'the man who brought the foreigners to Ireland'. This makes him one of the most controversial people in Irish history. Dermot was an unusual Irish king because he looked outside his country. In the 1140s he helped St Malachy to bring in improvements to the Irish Church. Twenty years later, when he was in political difficulties, he looked abroad for help and, by so doing, he opened Ireland up to the Normans.

A Opinions of Dermot after his death in 1171

A1 *The unknown author of* The Annals of Tigernach *wrote at the time*:

"Dermot Mac Murrough, king of Leinster, the man who destroyed Ireland after mustering the foreigners and after ruining the Irish, after plundering and razing churches and territories, died of an insufferable disease."

A2 *Gerald of Wales, a half-Welsh, half-Norman writer, wrote about Ireland not long after the Normans came:*

"Dermot was tall and well-built, a brave and warlike man among his people, whose voice was hoarse from constantly having been in the din of battle. He was obnoxious to his own people and hated by others. He preferred to be feared than to be loved."

1   Was the Irish writer pleased at Dermot's death? Why?

2   Did Gerald approve of Dermot? How does he give both his good and his bad sides?

3   Gerald was one of the Fitzgerald family which was given a lot of land in Ireland as a result of Dermot's invitation to the Normans. Might this have made him look with favour on Dermot? If so, how do you explain what he wrote in A3?

A3   Gerald describes Dermot after a victory over his Irish enemies:

"200 heads of his enemies were laid at Dermot's feet. He lifted up to his mouth the head of one he particularly loathed, and taking it by the ears and hair, gnawed at the nose and cheeks – a cruel and most inhuman act."

(From *Expugnatio Hibernica: The Conquest of Ireland*)

Not surprisingly Dermot was not a popular choice for a name among the Mac Murroughs after the twelfth century! There is a quite different opinion of Dermot in a letter written to him by St Bernard, the French abbot who was head of the Cistercian order of monks. In 1148 he wrote to praise Dermot for helping the building of churches and monasteries such as Baltinglass: 'It is really a great miracle in our opinion that a king at the end of the earth, ruling over barbarous peoples, should undertake works of mercy and great generosity'.

B Baltinglass Abbey, County Wicklow

4   The Abbey was built in a style spreading through England in the 1130s but new to Ireland. How might this have added to Irish writers' dislike of Dermot?

5   St Bernard calls the Irish 'barbarous people'. Whom do you think the Irish writer or Gerald of Wales would have called 'barbarous'?

6   How does one of the statements in A1 seem to be contradicted by Dermot's support for monastery building? Could both statements be true?

7   St Bernard refers to the Irish as being at 'the end of the earth'. Where have we come across similar phrases before? Bernard calls Dermot 'king of Ireland'. Was this true? Why do you think Bernard gave him this title?

Monasteries such as Baltinglass do not prove that Dermot was as glorious as St Bernard made him out. The Irish writers and Gerald may have written the truth about his bloodthirstiness. All we can say is that there were many sides to his character.

Dermot travels to Normandy

Dermot landed in Bristol in August 1166, but he had to travel as far as Aquitaine in the south of France before he found the man he was looking for. Henry II was king of England and ruler of a large part of France. He had been born in Normandy and spent more time in France than in England. Historians call Henry's lands 'the Angevin Empire' after the territory of Anjou from where his father came.

C The Angevin Empire in 1154

8 *Pick out Normandy, Anjou and Aquitaine on this map.*

9 *How does the map help to explain that Henry II may have taken a European view of the situation in Ireland?*

Did Henry want to conquer Ireland?

When Dermot caught up with the king he asked him for help to regain his lands in Ireland. In return Dermot accepted Henry as his lord. Henry was too busy to go to Ireland himself but he gave Dermot permission to recruit men in his lands to help him. Dermot returned to Bristol to look for supporters.

Henry II had become king of England in 1154 and in 1155 he had discussed plans to conquer Ireland with his advisers. He also sought the support of the Pope, Adrian IV. Adrian issued a letter or 'bull' called Laudibiliter which gave Henry permission to conquer Ireland.

D Adrian IV giving Henry II's ambassador permission to conquer Ireland

(From an Italian painting of about 1611)

10 *What does this scene suggest about the power of the pope in the twelfth century?*

Adrian IV was the only Englishman ever to become pope and the Irish later claimed that he was biased against them. It is more likely that Adrian issued Laudibiliter because he wished to see the Irish Church brought into line with the rest of Europe and thought Henry would be able to make sure this happened. Laudibiliter praises Henry 'for striving as a true Catholic prince should, to enlarge the boundaries of the church and to reveal the truth of the Christian faith to peoples still untaught and barbarous'. It was common in the twelfth century for European churchmen to criticise the Irish Church. Some Irish churchmen like St Malachy (see Unit 3) agreed with these criticisms. St Bernard, who was a Frenchman and a friend of St Malachy said the Irish were 'Christian in name but pagan in fact'. These men objected to the fact that priests in Ireland had wives, that they did not object when people went through a form of divorce and that Irish princes did not pay taxes, known as 'tithes', to the Church.

Questions and answers

We may now be able to give a fuller answer to the question 'why did the Normans come to Ireland?' We know that Henry II had been thinking of conquering Ireland before 1166 and we also know that he had the support of the Pope and other important churchmen. But the most important fact is that the Normans only came after they were invited in by Dermot. Only after their arrival did the conquest of Ireland become inevitable.

1 *Do you agree with the following description of the Norman invasion: 'Like most great changes in history it was an accident, unforeseen and unplanned'. Give reasons for your answer. Can you think of any other great historical event which happened by accident?*

2 *Dermot is a controversial figure. Where does the word 'controversial' come from and what does it mean? Can you think of any other controversial figures in Irish history? Explain your choice.*

3 *Does the fact that the Pope, St Bernard and St Malachy had a poor view of the Church in Ireland mean that Henry II wanted to conquer it to reform its Church? Can you suggest other reasons he might have had?*

5 Who were the first Norman invaders?

Dermot had been given permission by Henry II to recruit men from his kingdoms but it was up to him to find them. We know he succeeded but we need to ask where he found them, who they were and why they agreed to help him.

Dermot and Strongbow

1 *Why did the Normans find it difficult to conquer the other parts of Wales?*

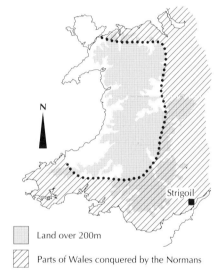

N

Strigoil

☐ Land over 200m

▨ Parts of Wales conquered by the Normans

The obvious place to look for soldiers to go to Ireland from Henry II's lands was in South Wales. For a hundred years since they landed in England, Normans had been trying to spread their rule in Wales. In the 1160s there were hundreds of castles where Norman lords and their knights ruled over the conquered lands. Many of the knights were the younger sons of lords and they were eager to find new lands to conquer because the Norman custom was that all a father's lands would pass to the eldest son.

Dermot first met the most powerful Norman lord in Wales. He was Richard FitzGilbert de Clare, Earl of Strigoil. He is better known to us as Strongbow. Strongbow had quarrelled with Henry II, who was suspicious of lords who had too much independence. Strongbow agreed to help Dermot to increase his power, which Henry II wanted to curb. In return, Dermot promised the hand of his daughter in marriage and agreed that Strongbow would succeed him as king of Leinster when he died.

Dermot then travelled on through South Wales to recruit knights. Many were keen to go once they heard that the powerful Earl of Strigoil had agreed to help. Dermot also knew what the knights wanted in return, telling them: 'Whoever shall wish for land or pence, I shall give them very ample pay, whoever may wish for soil or sod, richly shall I endow them'.

A South Leinster in 1170

2 *Suggest two reasons why the earliest Norman invaders landed in south Leinster rather than around Dublin.*

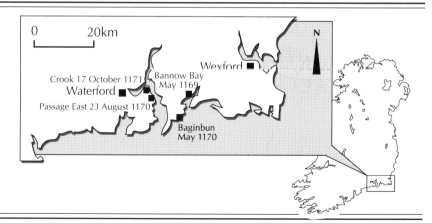

Dermot returned to Ireland in August 1167, after a year away. He brought only a handful of Normans with him so Rory O Connor did not see him as a great threat. Dermot submitted to Rory as his lord and was allowed to become master of some land in the Wexford countryside. Dermot bided his time until 1 May 1169 when 300 heavily-armed soldiers from South Wales landed at Bannow Bay. Dermot met them there and together they captured the town of Wexford. A year later another group of Normans arrived at Baginbun.

On 23 August 1170 Strongbow himself landed at Passage with 1000 men. He took command of the Normans who had come before and in a week they captured Waterford with much bloodshed. After the town's capture Strongbow and Aoife, Dermot's daughter, were married there. Strongbow next led the Normans to Dublin and captured it on 21 September 1170. In May 1171 Dermot died and Strongbow became ruler of Leinster, as the two men had agreed.

Henry II comes to Ireland

Henry II had been watching the growing power of the Normans in Ireland. One day this could be a threat to England. In England and Wales Strongbow had to accept Henry as king but in Ireland he might set up his own kingdom. Henry decided to come to Ireland himself with 4000 men and ordered Strongbow to meet him.

On 17 October 1171 the two men met at Crook. Strongbow told Henry that he had never planned to set up a kingdom for himself and surrendered his land in Ireland to the king. In return Henry allowed him to be lord over most of Leinster but not the towns of Wexford, Waterford and Dublin which the king kept for himself. To further ensure that Strongbow did not become too powerful Henry also granted lands to some of the men who had come over with him. The most important was Hugh de Lacy, who was granted the whole of the Irish kingdom of Meath which stretched from the east coast to the Shannon. This, Henry reckoned, would prevent Strongbow spreading his rule outside Leinster.

B A carving of Henry II from his tomb in France

3 *Why do you think Henry II would not allow Strongbow to keep the towns of Waterford, Wexford and Dublin?*

Who were the invaders?

It was less than five years since Dermot had visited Henry II. Now Dermot was dead the Normans in Ireland acknowledged Henry as their lord and the country was being invaded and conquered by a foreign army. We call these invaders 'Normans' but that does not really tell us a great deal about their nationality. One of the men who landed at Baginbun was Raymond le Gros (Raymond the fat). He said that among his followers there were 'French, English, Flemish, Welsh and Irish'. That is not surprising. French and English soldiers had taken part in the conquest of South Wales. Some of the conquered Welsh had taken service with them. Around 1100 some Flemish had come to South Wales from their home land of Flanders in modern Belgium. When we look at the great lords such as the de Clares or de Lacys it is difficult to know what nationality to give them as they had lands in Wales, Scotland, England and France.

1 *How different were the reasons of Henry II and Strongbow for coming to Ireland?*

2 *Should the Norman invasion be seen as a European or English operation?*

6 Did the Irish resist the Normans?

We saw in Unit 2 that Rory O Connor was the most powerful high-king that Ireland ever had. But when he died in 1198 the high-kingship was over. Most Irish kings and churchmen recognised the king of England as their overlord. How and why did this happen?

Rory and Strongbow

It was not easy for Rory O Connor to uphold his position as high-king. If he led armies to deal with every troublesome chief and king there would be no end to the fighting. It might also force some rebellious leaders to join against him. So Rory had good reasons for leaving them alone so long as they recognised him as high-king.

Rory did this to Dermot when he returned to Ireland in 1167. Dermot agreed to submit to him as high-king and in return Rory allowed him to keep some lands in Leinster. When the first Norman army came in 1169 and captured Wexford, Dermot again submitted to Rory as high-king and in return Rory recognised him now as king of all Leinster. It seems that Rory had not realised how serious a threat Dermot's Norman supporters were.

That became clear the next year when Strongbow arrived and captured Dublin. When Dermot died and Strongbow became king of Leinster Rory woke up to the danger and took a large army to recapture Dublin. Strongbow tried to bargain with him and said he would recognise Rory as high-king provided he could keep Leinster. Rory said he could keep Dublin, Wexford and Waterford but no other land. Strongbow was not going to give up Leinster so soon after becoming its king; he led his armies out of Dublin and they crushed Rory's army in September 1171. The following month Henry II arrived in Ireland.

The kings and the bishops choose

When Henry II landed the Irish kings turned their backs on Rory, the man they had once recognised as their high-king. They rushed to submit to Henry as their lord because they knew that he had come to stop Strongbow winning control over the whole country. Some may even have written to Henry asking him to come over and protect them against Strongbow.

The bishops also welcomed Henry II. One of the first things he did in Ireland was to call a church council of bishops and the leading abbots. They met in Cashel and passed a number of church laws which ordered changes in the Irish Church to bring it more into line with the Church in England and the rest of Europe. At the same time each bishop declared that he recognised Henry as lord of Ireland.

Henry II left Ireland on 17 April 1172. He never returned, but he remained watchful of what was happening in Ireland. In 1175 he made a treaty with Rory O Connor. It was written at Windsor, near London, and signed by Rory's ambassadors, including the Archbishop of Tuam.

A broken treaty

By the Treaty of Windsor Rory recognised that Henry was his lord for the whole of Ireland and accepted that he himself would no longer rule over the parts of Ireland which the Normans had already conquered. In return Henry recognised Rory as high-king of the rest of Ireland, but Rory still had to collect a tribute from the kings under him and pay it over to Henry.

The treaty was quickly broken by both sides. Rory was not strong enough to collect the tribute from the other Irish kings. They in turn saw the coming of the Normans as a chance to free themselves from Rory's control and refused to obey him. Even some of Rory's own family no longer accepted him as high-king.

On the other hand, Henry was too far away to stop the Normans in Ireland taking land from the Irish kings. Only a year after the treaty was signed John de Courcy led a band of Norman knights from Dublin to conquer the Irish kingdom of Ulaid, the eastern part of present-day Ulster (see Unit 13). Other Normans pressed into the Irish kingdoms of Thomond, Desmond and Munster and in 1177 Henry had to recognise them as lords of large parts of these Irish kingdoms.

A Ireland at the time of the Treaty of Windsor

1 *Here are some possible reasons for the Irish kings submitting to Henry. Take each one and discuss whether you think it is false, true or partly true.*

a) They did not think that Rory was strong enough to drive the Normans out.
b) They wanted to see English ways of life brought into Ireland.
c) They thought Henry would be able to control Strongbow.
d) They wanted to be sure they kept control of their own kingdoms.
e) They were traitors to Ireland.
f) They were more concerned with their own power than with joining together to drive the Normans out.

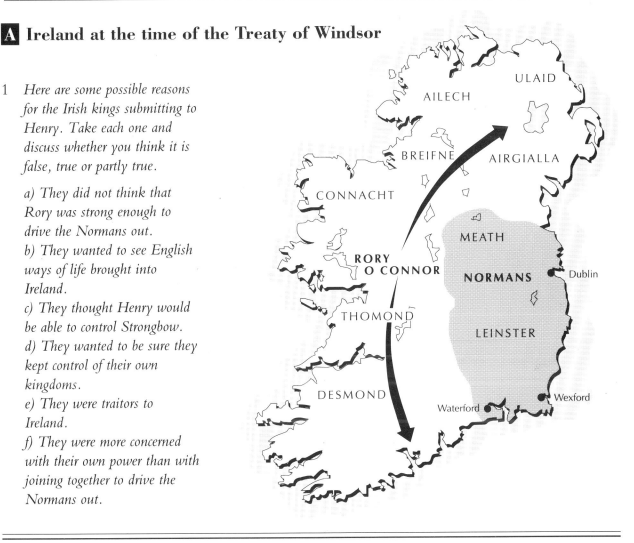

7 Why were the Normans so successful?

It took the first Normans just five years to control Ireland's most important cities on the east coast as well as the provinces of Leinster and Meath. Within seventy years, by 1240, they controlled two-thirds of the island. Yet they were always outnumbered by the Irish, so how are we to explain this success?

A Ireland in 1240

1 *How many years separate this map from the map of 1170? What had happened in these years?*

2 *What geographical reasons could you give for the fact that the Normans had not conquered the whole island?*

3 *In 1240 who controlled the best land, the Normans or the Irish?*

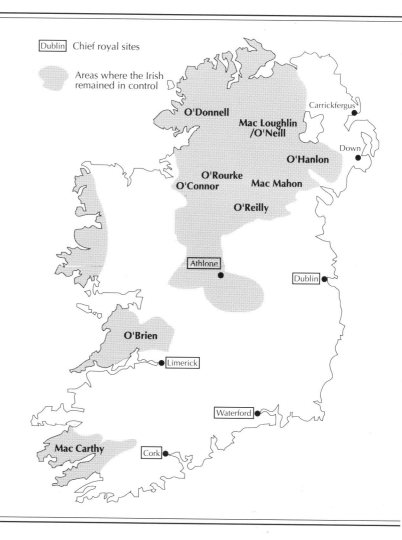

Dublin Chief royal sites

Areas where the Irish remained in control

O'Donnell

Mac Loughlin /O'Neill

Carrickfergus

Down

O'Hanlon

O'Rourke
O'Connor   Mac Mahon

O'Reilly

Athlone

Dublin

O'Brien

Limerick

Waterford

Mac Carthy   Cork

Warriors on horseback and on foot

The Normans' weapons and armour made it possible for them to win battles even when outnumbered. Their most powerful fighting force were knights who rode into battle wearing heavy armour and carrying lances. They also had archers (on horseback or on foot) and foot-soldiers who carried swords and shields. The knights had led the Norman armies to win much land throughout Europe.

Just after the Norman conquest of England a group of nuns made the Bayeux tapestry which told the story of the invasion. A hundred years later Gerald of Wales wrote a description of the Irish going into battle.

Gerald of Wales wrote that the Irish quickly learned to avoid battles on open ground where the knights could run them down. Instead they set ambushes for the invaders in the bogs and forests. Gerald recommended to the Normans that they use more archers to shoot down the Irish who were using slings to hurl stones at the knights.

B Knights in battle

4 *What weapons do the knights carry?*

5 *How does their armour appear to have been made?*

6 *Do you think their helmets were well designed for the jobs?*

(From the Bayeux tapestry)

C Irish warriors

7 *Draw a picture of Irish warriors going into battle.*

8 *Where might the Irish have a chance of winning?*

9 *Which sort of battles would the Normans win?*

"They regard weapons as a burden and they think it brave and honourable to fight unarmed. They use, however, three types of weapons – short spears, two darts and big axes which they have taken over from the Vikings. They are quicker and more expert than any other people in throwing stones as missiles and such stones do great damage to the enemy in an engagement."

(From Gerald of Wales *History and Topography of Ireland*, 1188)

If the Normans had relied only on their armies it is likely that the Irish could have driven them out eventually. For example, John de Courcy won three battles but lost two before he conquered Ulaid. So why did the Normans end up as rulers of most of the country?

One of the earliest invaders explained that 'we did not come for money but for land for ourselves and our children'. They showed that they intended to stay by building castles as soon as they were given land by Strongbow, by the king or by another great Norman leader. There was no time to build a stone castle at first so they put up a *motte*, which was the word the Normans used for mound of earth about 10 metres high and 20 metres across. The sides were steep and went down into a ditch where most of the earth for the motte had been dug. They built a wooden tower on top and put a fence on the outer edge of the ditch.

Most of the 'fairy mounds' scattered around our country today are really the remains of Norman mottes. They were put up not by fairies but by Irish people working under the watchful eye of Norman guards. Gerald of Wales explained how important the mottes were. The island would be brought under control, he wrote, 'by building castles everywhere in suitable places from coast to coast'. In 1186 an Irish writer noted that the country 'from the Shannon to the sea was full of castles and foreigners'. Like Gerald, he understood that mottes and Norman control went hand in hand.

D Remains of the Norman motte at Clonard

10 *How long would it take to build this with only picks, shovels and baskets to carry the earth in?*

11 *Imagine you are choosing a place to build a motte. What sort of place would you choose?*

1 *Knights were only a small part of Norman armies. Henry II brought 4000 men to Ireland in 1171 and only 500 of them were knights.*

a) Suggest reasons why knights were more expensive than archers or foot-soldiers.

b) Would the Norman armies have been successful if every soldier was a knight?

c) What was different about the social position of knights and other soldiers?

2 *The Irish preferred to ambush the Normans rather than to fight them on open ground. Can you think of a modern term for this type of warfare?*

8 How did the Normans affect the countryside?

The invaders were soldiers, but they were interested in more than fighting. They wanted to become rich from the lands they had conquered. This is why they had come to Ireland in the first place. Remember what Dermot promised them in 1166 when he was looking for their support (see Unit 5). What did the Normans do with the land they had conquered?

Fees and manors

When a great lord such as Hugh de Lacy was granted a huge area such as Meath he first divided the land among his most important supporters. These parcels of land were called 'fees'. A man held his fee in return for providing his lord with a fixed number of soldiers when the need arose. Sometimes the fee covered the same territory as one of the old Irish kingdoms.

A How Hugh de Lacy divided Meath

1 *Why did Hugh give land to Gilbert and Jocelin Nangle and Richard Tuite?*

"To Gilbert de Nangle
Hugh gives the whole of Morgallion,
To Jocelin he gave Navan
And the land of Ardbraccan,
To Richard Tuite likewise
He gave a rich fee . . ."

(From an early thirteenth-century poem)

Once a man such as Gilbert de Nangle or Jocelin had been granted his fee he first had to think about protection, so he would order a motte or castle to be built. When he was sure the fee was peaceful he would then choose the best land for the manor where the agricultural work was carried out under the eye of his bailiff.

How did a manor work?

The first requirement for his manor was peasants to work the land. When the Normans arrived many Irish peasants fled west, but they were encouraged to come back. These Irish peasants were called *betaghs*. Before the Normans they had been free, but on the manors they became the property of the lord who owned the land and could not use the common law to protect themselves or any property.

A large part of the manor was ploughed up to grow wheat, barley, oats and vegetables, which needed many more labourers than minding animals. The Normans soon found that there were not enough betaghs and they encouraged peasants from Wales or England to settle in Ireland. Some of these peasants had been unfree in England but in Ireland the Normans gave them their freedom. As free-men they were above betaghs in the eyes of the law, they had to pay rent for their land and they were often given fewer acres.

At the centre of the manor was the lord's residence, the manor house, which was often a castle. Usually this was surrounded by a small village with a church. Beyond were the fields, pastures and woodlands. There were a few very large fields which were divided into long narrow strips. The lord kept a number for himself as his *demesne*. The rest were shared out among the peasants. Each peasant's share was made up of strips in each field to make sure that everyone had some good and some poor land.

The peasants also owed 'labour service' to their lord. They had to work on his demesne land without being paid for it, usually for about fifteen days in the year. The betaghs had to do more for their lord than the free tenants. They had to find fuel for the lord's manor and to make his hay and stack it. They also had to grind their grain at the lord's mill – and pay for the privilege!

Although the fields were divided into strips each one had the same crop. Winter wheat was ploughed in a field one year and spring oats the next year. In the third year the field was left 'fallow' or idle. The fallow time prevented the soil being starved of the natural foods for the plants. Sheep and cattle were grazed on the pastures beyond the fields. Often there was woodland which provided timber and was a place for pigs to roam. Some manors also had orchards.

B Peasants working on a Norman manor in Ireland

2 *What are the peasants doing?*

3 *Oxen were used to pull the plough. How might this explain why fields were divided into long strips?*

4 *Most Norman manors in Ireland were in areas of lowland rather than in mountainous or boggy regions, why?*

1 *Many of the peasants who migrated to Ireland after the Norman invasion came from the west of England and the borders of Wales. Why do you think this was so?*

2 *If a betagh living in Meath had been ten years old in 1169 how might his life have changed by 1209 when he was fifty?*

How did the Normans change the economy?

The Norman manors produced corn, meat, wool and leather and often other things such as fish and timber. Most of these goods were eaten or used by the people of the manors but some was left over for trading. How did the Normans encourage trade? What goods were traded and where were they sold?

Infrastructure

Norman coin

It is said today that Ireland has difficulty in competing with other countries' industry and trade because our 'infrastructure' is weak. A country's infrastructure is said to be the things which help its business to run smoothly, such as its transport and banking systems.

The Normans made great improvements in Ireland's infrastructure. They cleared forests so that there was more farming land and they built roads and stone bridges to help traders. To encourage more trade, lords held fairs and markets on their manors.

The growth of trade could not have happened without an easy method of exchange so the Normans set up mints where metal coins were made for use around the country. By 1199 there were mints in Dublin, Carrickfergus and Downpatrick.

Town life

A The charter Henry II gave to Dublin

1 *What language was used in this charter? Why?*

2 *Which other Irish towns got charters like this?*

Unit 5 showed how the Norman conquest began with the capture of the Viking towns of Wexford, Waterford and Dublin. In 1172, soon after it was captured, Henry II granted Dublin a charter. This said the town was an independent borough which was not under the control of any Norman except the king. In other places the leading Normans founded new towns, usually near their strongest castles. Most of these became the large towns and cities of present-day Ireland. Some Normans set up a town on one of their manors. They gave craftsmen and merchants plots of land where they could build their homes, workshops and storehouses. Such a town was called a borough and the people who were given plots were its burgesses. The lord of the manor collected tolls from people who came to buy and sell in the borough. The burgesses did not have to do labour service for the lord of the manor. They ran the town's business themselves instead of being under the orders of the lord's bailiff or steward. The boroughs founded on manors are often only villages today.

Within the large towns the Normans saw to it that there was a guild of tradesmen or merchants to monitor the work. There was a guild for each business. A large town would certainly have guilds for butchers, bakers, vintners (winesellers), drapers or clothmakers and several more. These tradesmen often lived close together. In Dublin, for instance, the inn-keepers lived on Winetavern Street, the fast-food vendors on Cook Street and the fish sellers on Fishamble Street. The guilds set standards for the weights and measures of quality of goods; traders who broke the rules were expelled from the guild and then could not carry on their business. Guilds also laid down rules about how many apprentices there were to be and what they should be taught. Boys could only work in the guild's trade if they had seven years' apprenticeship with a member of the guild. Women were allowed to join guilds, but in many towns Irish people were not allowed to be members.

Most houses in the cities were made of wood with thatched roofs so there were many fires. Walls were thin so people had little privacy. Filth in the streets was a major problem. In 1489 a report to the king said: ' . . . dungheaps, swine, pigsties and other nuisances in the streets, lanes and suburbs of Dublin infect the air and cause death, fevers and disease'.

Trade

Wexford, Waterford and Dublin were the most important trading towns in the country, which was one reason why the Normans first set their sights on capturing them. Trade was easier by sea than overland and the Normans wanted to control Ireland's trade as a way of making money. The exports which brought most money into Ireland were wool, hides and fish.

The Normans also traded with more places in Europe than the Irish had previously. Wine came from France and Portugal. From Pisa in Italy Irish merchants got pepper and spices which had been grown in the Far East and brought to Italy by sea and overland. Wool from Ireland and England was sent to Bruges (in modern Belgium) where it was made into cloth, some of which was sold in Ireland.

B Ireland's ports and trade in the Middle Ages

C A rhyme of the Middle Ages

"Herring of Sligo and salmon of Bann
has made in Bristol many a rich man."

The title of this book is Ireland and the Normans: Progress or Decline? *Does this Unit describe progress or decline? Who in Ireland might think that the new Norman economy had damaged their way of life?*

10 How did the Normans govern?

The king of England was also the lord of Ireland. After Henry II left in 1172, however, only two more kings of England came to Ireland in the Middle Ages. King John came in 1210 and King Richard II came twice, in 1394 and 1399. With the lord of Ireland nearly always absent, how did the Normans govern the country?

The justiciar

The kings of England needed to be sure that the Normans in Ireland were obeying their commands so they always appointed one man to rule in their name. He was known as the king's *justiciar*. The king could send over one of his leading advisers to be justiciar or he could choose one of the Norman lords who lived in Ireland, or one of the leading churchmen there, such as the archbishop of Dublin.

The justiciar was commander-in-chief of the army in Ireland. It was his duty to lead the forces of the Normans against the Irish when they were at war. He was also the most important judge. If two powerful Norman lords argued, they came to him for justice. The justiciar was also the head of the civil service, which was divided into the chancery and the exchequer. The clerks in the chancery kept records of all the government's documents. The exchequer clerks collected the taxes and paid out money spent on carrying out the king's government. The head of the chancery was called the chancellor while the man in charge of the exchequer was the treasurer.

The sheriffs

The justiciar, chancellor and treasurer needed people to take charge of local affairs in every part of the country which the Normans ruled. So these parts of Ireland were divided, like England, into counties. Each county had a sheriff who was usually an important local man. He was responsible for law and order and held courts to decide local cases. It was also his duty to collect any money which people in the county owed to the government. The largest part of this money was the fines which guilty people had to pay but sometimes the government also ordered special taxes. There were some places where the money from fines did not go to the government but to a powerful lord. A district like this was known as a liberty.

Every year the sheriff had to travel to Dublin to hand over the money to the exchequer. The clerks of the exchequer sat at a table covered with a checkered cloth which they used as an abacus to count the money. If the sheriff did not produce the right amount he could find himself in gaol.

Parliament

The justiciar had a council to advise him. Before he could take some decisions, however, the justiciar needed to consult a wider body of men. The idea of calling parliaments sprang from this need for advice. The first Norman Parliament met at Castledermot in 1264.

A The Irish exchequer in action

1 *How do you think the exchequer got its name?*

2 *The clerks are at the back. How can you tell they are clerks?*

3 *On the left are two barons of the exchequer. What do you think their job was?*

4 *Which group of men is likely to contain the sheriffs?*

Norman parliaments had a House of Lords and a House of Commons. Bishops and abbots sat in the House of Lords as well as earls and barons. The House of Commons included all the sheriffs, but there were also two men from each county and from many of the towns or boroughs. Parliaments were powerful because the government could not call on people to pay taxes unless Parliament agreed.

Government on the move

Today many of the main departments of government are in Dublin or Belfast. In the Middle Ages the buildings of the chancery and treasury were usually in Dublin but the government was wherever the justiciar was. To be seen to be in charge of the country he was always on the move with a large staff of officials, soldiers and judges and they stayed for only a few nights at different castles, monasteries or large town houses. Wherever he was, he expected the local lords to meet him. The justiciar often called a meeting of Parliament outside Dublin. Other places where Parliament met were Drogheda, Castledermot, Trim, Clonmel, Cork and Limerick.

1 *Why did the justiciar pick these towns to hold parliaments?*

2 *Which parts of present-day government date back to the Normans?*

11 Did the Normans change the Irish Church?

Unit 4 told how the Pope supported Henry II's invasion of Ireland because Henry promised to bring the Irish Church into line with the rest of Europe. One part of the Irish Church was already changing – the monasteries. Before the Normans arrived new Orders such as the Cistercians and Augustinians had already opened some abbeys. However, the Irish bishops believed that Henry would push for other changes. How did the Normans try to change the Irish Church?

A From Gerald of Wales' book on Ireland

1 *What did the fishermen's reply tell Gerald about many Irish people?*

"When they were asked if they were Christians and baptised, they replied that they had never heard of Christ."

(From Gerald of Wales, *The History and Topography of Ireland*, 1188)

The parish

Gerald told the story of the two men to make the point that many Irish people had not heard the teaching of the faith. He thought the reason was that the Irish Church was not organised into parishes, each with its own priest. In Ireland, before the Normans came monasteries were the most important and wealthy part of the Church. Gerald believed that as a result the faith was not being preached to ordinary people.

It was the Normans who introduced the parish system we know today. For each manor the Normans also set up a parish with a priest and a church. To support the priest and his bishop everyone in the parish had to pay a tithe, which was a tenth of all they produced on their land.

A system of parishes required bishops with a large staff of priests and clerks who all needed an income to carry out their work. The king and the great Norman lords gave whole manors to the Church so that its bishops became lords of many manors. Half of the manors in the county of Dublin were held by the archbishop of Dublin and other churchmen.

New religious Orders

Many lords granted lands to religious Orders to build abbeys. They hoped that a gift to the service of God would help their souls if they arrived in purgatory. They also believed that monasteries would bring benefits to the people on their estates because the monks provided schools and hospitals.

2 *Who were the crusades fought against?*

3 *Many monks disliked friars. Why do you think this was?*

The Cistercians and Augustinians had already founded abbeys in Ireland before the Normans came and the first Normans opened many new houses for them. They also brought other Orders such as the Knights Templar and the Knights Hospitallar. These Orders had been founded during the crusades to protect Christian holy places in the Holy Land.

In the thirteenth century many lords in Ireland began to favour the friars. Like other landowners in Europe they had come to think that monks in monasteries gave less service to the people of the country than the Franciscans and the Dominicans who travelled among the people preaching and often lived in poverty.

Education

The parish clergy often had trouble making ends meet because the abbey which had appointed them took part of their tithe so they took on other jobs to help support themselves. We know of a priest in Smarmore, County Louth, who was also the local schoolmaster, vet and doctor. Education was not compulsory for children and usually only those who wished to become priests learned to read and write. The parish priest looked after their education.

B Slate used in the priest's school at Smarmore

4 *The priest at Smarmore taught his pupils music and how to translate between Latin and English. Why would they have found these lessons useful?*

5 *Teacher and pupils did their lessons on slate, writing with chalk. Why did they use these materials? What language do you think is on the slates?*

Students who wished to continue their studies beyond the parish school had to leave Ireland. In 1320 the Archbishop of Dublin tried to found a university in the city but nothing came of it. Instead students from Ireland went abroad, usually to Oxford. Perhaps the most famous of these students was a man called Richard FitzRalph who came from Dundalk. He became Chancellor of Oxford University and later Archbishop of Armagh.

The Normans greatly changed the Church in Ireland by bringing in parishes and new religious orders. However, this mostly happened in the parts of Ireland the Normans had conquered. There were, for instance, very few parishes in Connacht or the west of Ulster.

In which ways might the changes in the Church have made a difference to a betagh, or Irish peasant working on a Norman manor? Would he or she have benefited from any of them?

12 How did the Normans change building?

In Ireland today you can see hundreds of castles and churches built by the Normans, just as you can wherever they settled, from Sicily to Scotland. How were they built and what new fashions in building did the Normans bring to Ireland?

A Trim and Dundrum castles

(Trim was begun about 1170 and Dundrum around twenty years later)

---

1 *How had castle design changed and why?*

Large castles probably took twenty years to complete. At the centre of the castle was the keep where the lord and his soldiers lived. The earliest keeps were square but later ones were usually round. The keep was surrounded by an outer wall known as a 'curtain wall' which was high and thick enough to keep out enemy attackers.

If the king wanted a castle built in Ireland he would appoint a special 'keeper of the works' whose job it was to take charge of the workmen and buy the materials needed. One of these keepers was a man called William de Prene, who helped organise the building of Roscommon castle in the 1280s. In 1292 he was arrested for stealing building material, taking money he should have given to his carpenters and for faulty work on a bridge which collapsed.

Gothic buildings

The Normans had many new churches and monasteries built. Until around 1300 they usually sent for master-masons from England to take charge. They followed the European fashion known as 'Gothic' and often ordered local people to tear down an old building because they did not like the style. The master-masons often had stone shipped from quarries near Bristol.

B The church at Grey Abbey, a Cistercian monastery built in the 1190s

2 *What was similar about the shapes used in the different parts of Grey Abbey*

3 *What name is given to this style?*

After around 1300 Norman builders in Ireland stopped following English fashions. New master-masons no longer came over from England so the men who planned buildings came from Norman families, which by then had lived in Ireland for generations. There was little work for these master-masons in the fourteenth century as few new buildings were put up. In the fifteenth century, however, there was a boom in the Irish building trade. Small square castles known as 'tower houses' were built by the hundred. Many new priories for Dominican and Franciscan friars were also built. You do not see English stone in these buildings. Instead masons used Irish limestone which was tougher.

1 *How did the Normans regard the buildings they found in Ireland? How does this compare with their attitude to other aspects of Irish culture?*

2 *Why did it take so long to build castles and cathedrals?*

3 *These are some buildings which contain Norman remains. List any to be found in your town, parish or county. Is all of the building Norman, or just part of it? Motte; Castle; Tower house; Monastery; Church.*

13 The Normans in Ulster: An unlikely conquest?

This Unit looks at one particular part of the country, the Irish kingdom of Ulaid, which consisted of the modern counties of Down and Antrim. Who was the Norman who conquered it so easily in the 1170s? Why did Norman control later give way to the power of the O'Neills? Were the Normans a success or a failure in Ulster?

A The north and west of Ireland in the 1120s

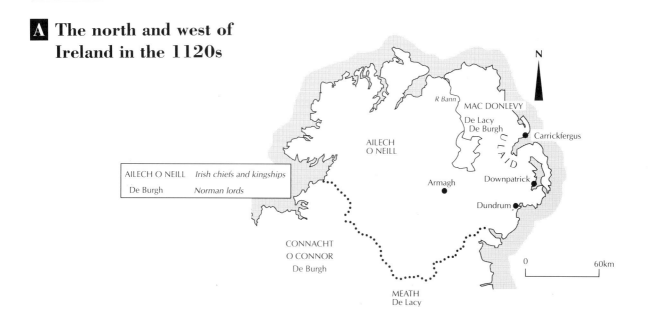

AILECH O NEILL — *Irish chiefs and kingships*
De Burgh — *Norman lords*

MAC DONLEVY
De Lacy
De Burgh
Carrickfergus
AILECH O NEILL
Armagh
Downpatrick
Dundrum
CONNACHT O CONNOR
De Burgh
MEATH De Lacy
R Bann
ULAID
0   60km

John de Courcy and his successors

Every people and country has its heroes. For the Normans in Ireland their hero was John de Courcy, the conqueror of the Irish Kingdom of Ulaid. Even while he was still alive he was portrayed as a hero by Gerald of Wales. Later, new stories were invented about de Courcy's deeds and added to those of Gerald. In the sixteenth century a descendant of the Normans in Ireland wrote of John that 'he was one of the strongest men that then was in Europe. The valientest, the fairest, the soberest, the wisest, the fiercest in Europe was not his like'. Why was John thought to be so remarkable?

The answer is that John achieved great successes with very little backing in Ireland. He was a 'self-made man' and the Normans loved this kind of spirit. He came from an unimportant family in Somerset in the west of England and arrived in Dublin in 1176 to make his fortune. With a small force he set out to conquer the Irish kingdom of Ulaid. Despite being outnumbered by the Irish he soon succeeded in making himself master of the area and ruled almost as a prince. He married a princess from the Isle of Man and had coins minted with his name on them. He also showed devotion to Irish saints such as Patrick and Colm Cille so that the Irish would grow to accept his rule. He even changed the name of the town of Down to Downpatrick.

John also brought Norman styles to his conquered lands. In the last Unit we saw how the invaders brought the Gothic style of architecture to Ireland. John de Courcy used it in two of the Cistercian houses he founded, Grey Abbey and Inch Abbey. He also built castles such as Carrickfergus and brought in tenants such as the Logans, Savages, Russels and Hackets whose descendants are still found in Ulster today.

B Inch Abbey

1 *What is the name of the style of this building? How do you recognise it?*

2 *Why would de Courcy have minted his own coins? Why might this have worried the king of England?*

The rise of the O Neills

John de Courcy's success and power made the king of England, King John, suspicious of him. In 1204 the king had him driven out and replaced with Hugh de Lacy II, the son of the Hugh de Lacy who had conquered Meath. He was made the first earl of Ulster. He died without a son to follow him and so the earldom of Ulster was next given to the family of de Burgh.

The de Burghs pushed west from Down and Antrim across the Bann into the centre of modern Ulster. They built new towns and castles but they could not control the surrounding countryside. This part of the north was the stronghold of the O Neills who were supported by many lesser Irish chiefs. The O Neills and their allies were ready to accept the de Burghs as their lords and pay rent to them, but they would not give up their land to be turned into Norman-style manors and their people continued to live and farm in the Irish ways.

King John had also allowed the de Burghs to conquer most of Connacht so the Normans were threatening the O Neills from both sides. The O Neills began to resist. They stopped paying rent for their lands to the Norman lords and encouraged the other Irish chiefs to do the same. In the 1250s Brian O Neill persuaded O Brien of Thomond and O Connor of Connacht to support him as high-king. The Irish in the north and west went to war with the Normans. The fighting came to an end when the Normans won the Battle of Downpatrick in 1260. Brian was killed and his head sent to England.

In 1315 Brian's son, Donal O Neill, built up a stronger force to face the Normans. He invited Edward Bruce to come from Scotland with an army and become high-king. It was a good time to do this because Edward's brother was Robert Bruce the king of Scotland and the year before he had defeated the English army in battle at Bannockburn in central Scotland.

Edward never became high-king because he was killed in battle near Dundalk in 1318. But the Scots had helped the O Neills to weaken the power of the earls of Ulster. In 1333 the de Burgh Earl of Ulster was murdered by some of his own men. It was another blow to the de Burghs. The Earl had no sons and the earldom passed through daughters to their husbands who usually lived in England and did not defend their lands. The de Burghs who still ruled parts of Connacht became more and more like their Irish neighbours and less like Norman lords in the eastern parts of Ireland.

With the Norman earls out of the way the O Neills became the greatest power in the whole of Ulster. They made the other Irish chiefs accept their troops onto their land just as the Norman Earl of Ulster had done. Norman settlers were forced out of most of Down and Antrim and were left with just the Ards peninsula and Carrickfergus. Here they were cut off from the rest of the settlers in Ireland and most of them adopted Irish customs, although the townsmen of Carrickfergus continued to look for Norman help against the Irish.

Armagh

The man who held the position of archbishop of Armagh often helped bring peace between the Irish and the Normans. He was not usually Irish and lived in County Louth, which was controlled by the Normans, rather than in Armagh, which was ruled by the Irish. Despite this the Irish showed the archbishop great respect. In the fifteenth century archbishops of Armagh even attended the inauguration ceremonies of the O Neills in Tyrone when they were proclaimed kings. This helped to protect the Normans in Ulster from Irish attacks.

1 *Why do you think that the conquest of Ulaid seemed more unlikely in 1176 than the conquest of Leinster, Meath or Munster? Why did Ulster become a major centre of resistance to the Normans?*

2 *If the Irish respected the archbishops of Armagh why do you think the archbishops still preferred to live in Louth rather than Armagh city?*

14 Who resisted the Normans?

The Normans only ever conquered about two-thirds of Ireland. In the 1250s the O Neills and other Irish lords began to try to regain control of parts of the country and after 1300 the area ruled by the Normans actually began to shrink. Why did the chiefs rally behind men like the O Neills against the Normans? How successful were they?

Broken promises

In the 1175 Treaty of Windsor, Henry II had agreed that there would be no more Norman conquests in Ireland and Rory agreed to recognise the king as his overlord. The treaty was broken only two years later when John de Courcy conquered Ulaid and the king did nothing to stop him. Even so, most Irish chiefs and kings believed that the best way of keeping the Normans out of their lands was to accept the English king as their overlord. When King John came to Ireland in 1210 twenty of them went to Dublin to do homage by kneeling before him and swearing loyalty.

The Irish wanted to be able to say that they held their lands from the king in the same way as the Norman lords. But these Norman lords would not accept this. They were a conquering people who regarded the people they conquered as inferiors. An important sign of this was that the Normans would not allow the defeated people to use the same law as themselves.

An Irish person was not free to take a Norman, English or Welsh settler to court and accuse him of stealing his land or possessions. If a settler murdered another settler he was executed, but if he murdered an Irishman he might only have to pay a fine. Among themselves the Irish were allowed to use their own law known as Brehon law, even though one English king, Edward I, said that 'the laws which the Irish use are detestable to God and so contrary to all laws that they ought not to be called laws'.

The English viewed all the Irish in the same way when it came to English law, whether they were betaghs living on Norman manors or great kings. In 1276 the Archbishop of Cashel, who was an Irishman, asked the king to grant English law to the Irish. The Norman barons in Ireland objected because this would make the Irish people their equals. The king took their side although he said that an Irishman with enough money could buy a charter which allowed him to use English law.

Resistance

The Irish kings who took most care to show loyalty to the English king were the O Connors of Connacht. In the end this did them no good. As we saw in Unit 13, King Henry II gave the de Burghs permission to conquer their lands. This forced the O Connors and O Briens to rally behind the O Neills. It was the beginning of many years of Irish resistance to the Normans. We have a good idea of how strongly the Irish felt from a letter that Donal O Neill wrote to the Pope asking for his help in 1317. The letter is called the *Remonstrance*, which means protest. In it Donal accused the Normans of persecuting the Irish and treating them unfairly in law.

A The Remonstrance

1 *How might the Normans reply to the charge that they put the Irish under slavery?*

2 *Which right mattered most to lords such as the O Neills?*

"In order to throw off the cruel and intolerable yoke of their slavery and to recover our native liberty we are forced to make war to the death against them, impelled to put our manhood to the test of war in defence of our rights rather than submit any longer like women to their appalling outrages."

The defeat and death of Edward Bruce in 1318 ended the attempts of the O Neills to unite the Irish under their leadership and drive the Normans from Ireland. But the resistance of the Irish since the 1250s was important because it stopped the spread of Norman power. From that time on the Normans had to accept the fact that not all the Irish would be beaten. The story of the resistance also shows that the Irish had one new strength and one important weakness.

The new strength was that from the 1250s the Irish had soldiers fighting for them who were as tough as the Normans. These soldiers were heavily-armed fighters from the western isles of Scotland. They were called *galloglass*, from the Irish *gall oglaich* for foreign warriors. Galloglass first came with a Scottish princess who married one of the O Connors. Others followed them to different parts of Ireland where they came to an arrangement to fight for an Irish chief in return for land. The names of some of these galloglass families who settled on Irish land are still found today; names such as Mac Sweeney, Mac Cabe, Mac Donald and Sheehy.

The main Irish weakness was that they did not unite against the Normans. People like the O Neills thought that the best way of uniting was to have a strong high-king. Other chiefs would never agree to this because it meant giving up some of their own power. Many Irish writers criticised Donal O Neill for inviting Edward Bruce to Ireland because of the damage his army caused in the countryside.

B

B1 *Galloglass*

3 Why would the galloglass be able to stand up to the Norman knights better than the Irish soldiers had done when the Normans first arrived?

4 Compare the galloglass of the thirteenth century with what Gerald of Wales wrote about the Irish warriors in the twelfth century (Unit 7). Does this help to explain the idea that they brought new strength to the Irish?

5 Throughout history people have travelled between Ireland and Scotland. The galloglass who settled here in the Middle Ages spoke Irish and fitted in easily with Irish society. Think of other examples of people travelling between Scotland and Ireland.

B2 *Norman knight*

From what you have read about the Normans in Ireland, do you think:

a) The Irish would not have resisted so strongly if they had been granted English law?

b) It was lack of unity among the Irish which brought the Normans to Ireland in 1169 and lack of unity which broke up Irish resistance in the 1300s?

Give reasons for your answer.

15 Beyond Norman rule: What was Ireland like?

Large parts of Ireland were never colonised by the Normans. As time went by more land fell into Irish hands. How did life in these areas differ from life in parts under Norman control?

'The best and most perfect in the world'

We saw in Units 2 and 3 that when the Normans came the customs of the Irish were different from those of other people in Europe and that the Irish were proud of this fact. Two centuries later this was still true. In the 1390s a Spanish knight on a pilgrimage to Lough Derg in Donegal met Niall O Neill, the chief of the Irish of Ulster. O Neill wanted to hear of the customs of the Spanish and French but he ended by telling the knight that the ways of the Irish were still 'the best and most perfect in the world'.

In some important ways the arrival of the Normans made Irish society even less like the rest of Europe than it had been before. One example was the way in which the Irish thought about government. Before the invaders came, the kings of small kingdoms were beginning to accept the leadership of the king of their province. The Normans saw the power of these provincial kings as an obstacle to their conquest and encouraged the smaller kingdoms to become independent again. This meant that they often quarrelled among themselves. The more that the Irish chiefs quarrelled the better it was for the Normans.

A An Irish poet's view

1   *What policy does the poet suggest the Irish should follow?*

"Eire is ruined by rivalry among the Irish;
mutual love in peace is not their policy;
their anger keeps them apart;
sad they cannot agree."

(Aoughus Oh Eoghusa)

Irish lordships

As the rivalry between small kingdoms went on, their kings began to see themselves more as war-lords than law-makers. They stopped calling themselves *ri* which means 'king' and instead they used the term *taoiseach* which means 'chieftain'. When a taoiseach was chosen he was inaugurated at a traditional site, with ceremonies which dated back to pre-Christian times.

The taoiseach was chosen from a family group which included brothers, cousins, uncles, nephews, sons, grandsons and even more distant relatives. The eldest son or brother of the dead lord did not automatically succeed him, as happened among the Normans. With such a wide group to choose from it is not surprising that branches of the same family were often at war with each other.

The new chief had been elected by the members of his family, not by the people he now ruled over. To keep his hold on power he had a private army of galloglass. The peasants had to provide these soldiers with food and shelter.

Each lord also appointed a judge or *brehon* to decide law cases in his lands. The post of brehon was hereditary, which means that it passed to a man's son or his nephew. The most important of these legal families were the Egans and the Clancys. Each lordship also had its hereditary doctors such as the Hickeys and the Cassidys, hereditary musicians like the Duignans and hereditary poets such as the Dalys and Higginses. The medical families often sent their sons to England, France or Italy for their education.

The Irish outside the Norman areas had no need for coinage. Although they did grow crops, cattle were more important to them and battles between Irish chiefs usually involved cattle raids. The Irish did not live in towns and built few stone buildings. Chiefs lived on a *crannog*, a house on an island in the middle of a lake, or in hill-forts. People moved from one place to another within their lordship as they grazed their cattle on new pastures or else led them to safe places, away from an enemy raid.

B Crannog, Cloonacleigh Lough, County Sligo

2 *How would a chief have reached the crannog?*

3 *Would his enemies have known how?*

4 *Why would a chief choose to live on a crannog or hill-fort?*

1 *Explain how the break-up of the Irish areas into small lordships helped the Normans stay in control in much of the country.*

2 *List the people you know whose ancestors were judges, doctors, poets, musicians and Scottish mercenaries.*

16 Did the Church unite the two nations in Ireland?

Unit 4 explained that reform of the Church was one of the reasons why Pope Adrian IV granted *Laudibiliter* to Henry II. The Normans and the Irish shared the same Christian religion so we would imagine that the Church helped to bring the two nations together. Was this what happened?

The bishops

In all the countries they ruled, the Normans used the Church as a main part of their system of government. Abbots and bishops were often senior government officials such as chancellors, treasurers and even justiciars. The men who served them were lesser priests called *clerks*. The Church controlled nearly all the schools and the few people who could read and write usually took holy orders as clerks. Clergy were useful as officials because they could not marry and so they could not keep a government position in their family.

Because they relied so heavily on the Church, the Normans in Ireland wanted bishops to be their own men, rather than Irishmen. Twice in the thirteenth century the English king ordered that no Irish man should be a bishop. In fact, the Irish bishops had always supported the Normans in Ireland in the hope that they would reform the Church. In practice the king could not stop Irishmen becoming bishops in areas not controlled by the Normans.

The monasteries

When a Norman lord was granted land in Ireland one of the first things he would do was found a monastery near his castle. Lords gave land to these new monasteries rather than to the older Irish monasteries which had been founded before the conquest. The monks in the new houses would be Norman, not Irish.

Trouble arose where there was already an Irish monastery in the district. The Cistercian house of Mellifont, near Drogheda was set up by St Malachy in 1142, but the area was conquered by the Normans. In the early thirteenth century the monks of Mellifont, who were Irish, were accused of not following the rules of the Cistercian Order. The Normans laid down that the abbot could not be Irish and allowed only Irishmen who could speak French and Latin to become monks. The Irish deeply resented this attack on their language and learning.

The Irish Church

The Normans said that they had come to Ireland to bring the Irish Church into line with the rest of Europe. This did happen in the parts of the country they conquered, but wherever the Irish kept control the Church was very different. Priests often married and abbots passed on the position from father to son. In the same way as we saw that certain families specialised in the law or poetry there were also priestly families.

Eoin O Grady was Archbishop of Cashel from 1332 to 1345. His son, also called Eoin, was Archbishop of Tuam from 1365 and 1371. This man's son, Seán, was also Bishop of Elphin (Roscommon) from 1407 to 1417. Sometimes property which belonged to the Church came to belong to families of priests instead. This did not happen among the Norman priests in Ireland.

In the areas ruled by the Normans, European ways of worship became common. In the Irish areas this did not happen. At first, the Irish bishops were eager for the Normans to bring their Church into line with Europe but their view changed when it became clear that the invaders did not trust Irish bishops.

Pilgrimages

One way in which religion brought the two sides together was through pilgrimages. The most popular place of pilgrimage in medieval Europe was the shrine of St James at Santiago in northern Spain. Norman and Irish pilgrims made the long and dangerous sea-journey together from Ireland.

A Pilgrimages

A2 *A souvenir for pilgrims*

A1 *Pilgrim routes to Santiago*

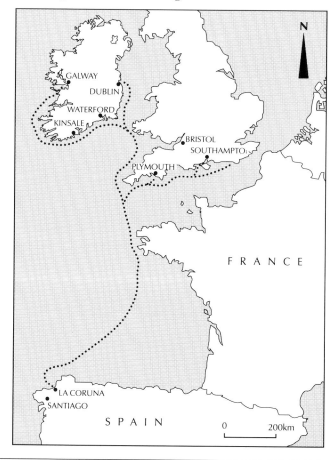

A3 *An unknown English pilgrim wrote about sleeping near the bilge pump*

"When we went to bed
the pump was near our head
a man would be better off dead
than to smell thereof the stink."

---

1 *Did the Norman invasion strengthen or weaken the Church?*

2 *Suggest ways in which the lives of an Irish and a Norman bishop in Ireland might differ?*

17 How did the Irish view the English?

The men who invaded in 1170 were mostly descended from the French-speaking Normans who had conquered England in 1066. As time went on they began to describe themselves as English. What did the Irish dislike about them and what did they admire them for? Did contact with the English change any parts of Irish culture?

Irish attitudes

It is easy to find documents which suggest that all the Irish always hated all the English. Some examples are given below. But they do not give the whole picture. Many Irish and English lived alongside each other peacefully. Some Irish like the historian in D were not ashamed to write about their admiration for their neighbours.

A The Irish view of the Normans

1 *What reason does O Neill give for 'natural hostility'?*

"We have natural hostility to each other arising from the ceaseless slaying of fathers, brothers, nephews and friends so that we can have no inclination to friendship in our time or in that of our sons."

(From Donal O Neill's Remonstrance to the Pope, 1317)

B An Irish poet's view of the English

2 *What has happened to the man?*

Thomas, son of O Reilly, a chief from Cavan is said to have written:

"The cry of the Englishwoman over the Englishman
that is the cry I do not lament
bright and melodious it is for me
that the Englishwoman wails."

C An outsider's view

3 *What impression do A, B and C give of the feelings between the Irish and English?*

4 *Might the same things have been written if the invaders had been from Holland or Hungary?*

". . . the two nations persecute each other with an insatiable hatred."

(The German Archbishop of Armagh in the 1240s)

D A historian's view

"The chiefs of Erin prospered under those princely English lords who gave up their foreignness for a pure mind, their surliness for good manners, their stubbornness for sweet mildness and their perverseness for hospitality."

(A Galway historian in the fourteenth century)

Borrowing from the English

One of the first things that Strongbow did in Ireland was to marry Dermot Mac Murrough's daughter. Intermarriage like this happened often so that many children had both English and Irish parents. Irish and Norman children would often be brought up together because many lords preferred to have their children brought up by foster-parents.

The most obvious way in which the Irish borrowed from the English was in the names they gave to their children. We read about people called 'Ralph Mac Mahon', 'Edmund O Kennedy', 'Henry O Neill' and 'William O Kelly'. The Christian names were first used by the Normans but became popular with the Irish.

The Irish did not build in stone to the same extent as the Normans, but this did not mean that they never did. In the areas where Irish chiefs drove the English out they took over their castles for their own use. They also built their own. This was especially true in the fifteenth century. Small castles called tower houses were built throughout Ireland and it is impossible to tell whether they were for English or Norman lords.

E A tower house built by an Irishman in County Galway

5 *Was this built for comfortable living or for defence? How do you know?*

6 *Why might an Irish chief feel he needed a home like this?*

Brehon law grew closer to English law. It took over English legal terms such as *aturnae* which means 'attorney' and *seiceduir* which means 'executor' (the person who deals with the will of a dead person). In law, as in other aspects of life, the Irish remained different from the English and were proud of it, but they also copied and used ideas which they found useful.

1 *Why would Irish chiefs wish to borrow some customs from the English? Would it strengthen or weaken their position with their own people?*

2 *Why did your parents choose your name? Think of the Christian or first names of the people in your class. What influences do they reveal?*

18 More Irish than the Irish themselves? (1)

In the last four units we have seen the effects the Norman invasion had on the Irish. In the next two we look at how the English in Ireland were changed by their contact with the Irish. By the middle of the fourteenth century some settlers were complaining that Irish ways were gaining the upper hand. What were they worried about?

The retreat of the conquest

At the very beginning of the Norman conquest Gerald of Wales wrote about four Irish prophets who had said that almost all of the English would be driven out, but they would hold on to parts of the country near the east coast. Gerald's forecast turned out to be a fairly accurate description of Ireland 300 years later. English customs were strongly rooted in Leinster and Meath which had taken the greatest number of English settlers. In other parts of Ireland the invaders had never persuaded enough English peasants to work on the manors they set up.

In the early fourteenth century two natural disasters weakened the position of the settlers. The first was the worst famine to hit Europe in the Middle Ages. It happened between 1315–18, just at the time when Edward Bruce and his Scottish troops were also ravaging the country. There were reports of cannabilism. A writer in Connacht reported that 'undoubtedly men ate each other in Ireland' at this time. In Dublin a monk wrote 'women ate their children from hunger'. The second disaster was the plague, known as the 'Black Death' which swept through Europe and wiped out at least a quarter of its population. At the end of 1348 the Black Death reached Ireland.

A A Franciscan in Kilkenny on the plague

1 How does the first sentence give a good idea of what the word 'contagious' means?

"This pestilence was so contagious, that those who touched the dead or persons sick of the plague were straightaway infected themselves and died. Many died from boils and ulcers and running sores which grew on the legs and beneath the armpits while others suffered pains in the head and went almost into a frenzy, while others spat blood."

In 1350 the Archbishop of Armagh, told the Pope that while the plague had not killed many Irish it had wiped out more than two-thirds of the English in Ireland. He was exaggerating but it is true that the Black Death killed a bigger proportion of English because the settlers lived in manors and towns while the Irish lived in smaller scattered groups. Many manors became deserted. In some places the Irish began to win back land from the English and in others English people began to take on Irish ways.

After the Black Death the settlers felt under so much pressure that they asked King Edward III to send over a powerful leader to help them. In 1361 the king's son, the Duke of Clarence arrived. In 1365 he called a Parliament at Kilkenny which passed a series of laws or 'statutes'.

B Deserted medieval village, County Tipperary

2 *What do the lines in the photograph represent?*

3 *Was this a big village?*

4 *What happened to the villagers?*

C The first part of the Statutes of Kilkenny

5 *What changes did the Parliament see in the life of many English settlers between the 1170s and the 1360s?*

6 *The third part gives the main reason why the Statutes were passed. How would you explain it in your own words?*

"At the conquest of Ireland and for a long time after, the English there used the English language, dress and manner of riding, and they and their subjects called 'betaghs' were governed by English law.

But now many English there live by the manners, fashion and language of the Irish enemies and have made marriages and alliances with them.

As a result the land and its people, the English language, loyalty to the king and English law are in decline and the Irish enemies are raised up, contrary to right."

The Statutes of Kilkenny tried to forbid the settlers taking up Irish customs. There was to be no more marriage with the Irish. English children were not to be fostered with Irish families. The English were to speak English, use an English name, look, dress and ride their horses like Englishmen. They were not to use Irish law. Irish minstrels were not to be patronised and Irishmen were not to be allowed into monasteries in English areas.

The Statutes of Kilkenny could not stop the English becoming more Irish for one very good reason. There were not enough settlers any more and many of those who survived the Black Death were migrating back to England.

1 *Why might an Englishman marry an Irishwoman or foster his children with an Irish family? What might such an Englishman say in his defence when he heard about the Statutes of Kilkenny?*

2 *Until very recently laws in South Africa tried to keep the races apart. Can you think of the name of this system? Do you think it could be applied to the Statutes of Kilkenny?*

19 More Irish than the Irish themselves? (2)

It would have been surprising if the English had not been influenced by Irish culture. The two nations married each other and traded with each other as well as fighting with each other. To what extent did the settlers lose their English identity and become Irish?

Gaelicisation

A A fifteenth-century de Burgh

1 *Which features of this man's appearance and weapons are Irish and which Norman or English?*

2 *Is he an Irish chief or a Norman lord?*

3 *Look back at what the historian from Galway said about the 'chiefs of Erin' and the English lords in Unit 17. Might he have had the de Burghs (later, often known as the Burkes) in mind?*

The de Burghs were one of the most important Norman families in Ireland. They conquered Connacht in 1235 and later became earls of Ulster (See Units 13 and 14). After the last de Burgh earl of Ulster was murdered in 1333 the branch of the family which ruled land in Connacht became cut off from the English government in Dublin and set about building-up its own local power. By the fifteenth century it was difficult to tell them apart from the Irish chiefs around them. They spoke Irish, dressed like them and rode their horses in the Irish way. They chose their chiefs and inaugurated them in the same manner. They used Irish law and employed Irish poets to glorify them in their poems.

The word we use to describe what had happened to the de Burghs is 'gaelicisation'. Other Norman families (such as the Barrys in Cork and the Dillons in Westmeath) became as gaelicised as the de Burghs. Some did not go so far, but they did adopt parts of the Irish culture. The most important Norman families in the fifteenth century, the

FitzGeralds of Kildare and the Butlers of Ormond (Kilkenny and Tipperary), could speak Irish, had poems written to them in Irish and used Irish law when it suited them. They also intermarried with the Irish. However, they did not break their links with the English government in the way that the de Burghs did.

There was much less gaelicisation in the cities and on the eastern coast. Here the English were more numerous and continued to regard the Irish and their ways as inferior. They passed laws to keep the races apart. If an Irishman wished to live in a city he had to buy a charter giving him English law. There was even an attempt to make the two peoples look different. Because Irishmen generally grew moustaches a law was passed saying that an Englishman 'must have no hair upon his upper lip, so that the said lip be shaven at least once every two weeks'.

The middle nation

It would be wrong to think that gaelicisation meant that the settlers considered themselves to be Irish. Irish poets used the word *gaill* 'foreigners' to describe the English in their poems and this suited the settlers very well. They had no intention of letting the Irish forget that the English were the descendants of a conquering race who had beaten the Irish and won most of the country. Gerald of Wales's account of the conquest of Ireland was a popular book among them because it told of the deeds of their ancestors.

There is a story in Gerald's book which helps us to understand how the settlers looked upon themselves. He tells us about a speech made by Maurice, one of the first settlers of the FitzGerald family who later became the earls of Kildare. Maurice and other Normans were besieged in Dublin by Rory O Connor. Maurice spoke to the others, saying: 'Surely we do not look to our own people for help? To the Irish we are English, but to the English we are Irish. The people of both islands hate us equally.' In the Remonstrance that Donal O Neill sent to the Pope in 1317 we can find a special name that the English in Ireland had for themselves. Donal says that they called themselves 'the middle nation'. He meant that they saw themselves as different from the English in England as well as from the Irish.

1 *Adoption of Irish ways is called 'gaelicisation'. We saw that the Irish also adopted some English ways. What word would describe this?*

2 *'History shows that it is not only senseless and cruel, but also difficult to state who is a foreigner' (Claudio Magris). The man who wrote this was thinking of central Europe where people with different languages and cultures have arrived over the centuries and now live together. Do you think his words hold true for medieval Ireland? Were the settlers really still foreigners after living here for 300 years?*

20 The 'English by blood' and 'by birth': Friend or foe?

Irish poets called the Normans who settled in Ireland *gaill* which means 'foreigner', and those who lived in England *Saxain* which means 'Saxons'. They saw that there were differences between the two groups. The English recognised this as well. The descendants of the Normans who settled in Ireland came to be called 'English by blood' while those who were born and lived in England were called 'English by birth'. There were sharp disputes between the two groups. What caused them and how serious were they?

English clowns and Irish dogs

In 1324 the Irish Parliament met in Kilkenny. A dispute broke out between Arnold Power and the local bishop, Richard Ledred. Arnold was a Norman lord from Kilkenny. In other words he was 'English by blood'. Bishop Richard had only recently arrived from England where he has been born and educated. So he was 'English by birth'. Arnold tried to turn the Parliament against Richard. He called him 'a foreigner from England' and said that he had insulted Ireland. He went on to say that 'the disgrace of this country touches every one of us'.

The strong words show two important things. 'English by blood', like Arnold Power, looked on the 'English by birth' as outsiders. They also felt a loyalty for Ireland, the country where they had been born and brought up. Arnold, for instance, proudly reminded the Parliament that 'the land of Ireland has usually been called an "isle of saints"'. But this did not mean that the English by blood had given up on the English connection. They still expected help from England in their difficulties with the Irish. The settlers on the east coast and in the towns of Ireland were particularly anxious to keep these links alive.

In the 1360s they begged the king for help. He sent his son Lionel, Duke of Clarence, with a large army from England, but rows soon broke out between the soldiers and the settlers. They were meant to be on the same side fighting the Irish, but they quarrelled with each other instead. At one stage Lionel forbade anyone born in Ireland to enter his camp, which was a great insult to the English by blood.

One of the Statutes of Kilkenny tried to solve the problem. It laid down that in future no difference was to be made between the English born in Ireland and the English born in England. The two sides were also to stop insulting each other. The settlers were to stop calling people from England 'English clowns' while those who had come from England were to stop calling the settlers 'Irish dogs'.

The English in Ireland would have been annoyed at being called 'Irish'. They were always reminding the king that there were two nations in Ireland; the Irish who were the king's enemies and the English – that is, themselves – who were his loyal subjects. This was true even for families like the de Burghs who spoke Irish and lived in the Irish manner but still considered themselves English not Irish.

What the settlers especially hated was being treated as foreigners if they ever went to England. In 1440 anyone living in England who had been born in Ireland was declared to be an 'alien' or foreigner and had to pay a special tax. This rule was only changed after the Parliament in Ireland objected.

A buttress and a post

The English by blood believed that the king of England neglected them and might even abandon them though he was also lord of Ireland. In fact English kings knew well the dangers of letting Ireland slip from their grasp.

A A poem written for King Henry VI in 1437

1   *What is a buttress?*

2   *How was Ireland a buttress and a post for England?*

3   *How might Ireland be lost to the king?*

"Keep Ireland that it be not lost
for it is a buttress and a post
under England."

The poet was saying that England could break up if the buttress and post were taken away. There had been times when this was a real fear. The English remembered that the Scots, under Edward Bruce, had invaded Ireland in 1315. What if the French, who were more powerful than the Scots, were to do the same? What if a rival to the king of England was able to use Ireland as a power-base? In the long run it suited both the English by blood and the English by birth to stay on the same side, despite their dislike for each other.

---

1   *If one of the English by blood went to England what would an Englishman living in England have found noticeable about him?*

2   *If the English by blood were proud of Ireland why do you think they did not want to be called Irish?*

3   *Can you think of any other time in history when Ireland might have been a 'buttress' supporting England or else a back door through which England's enemies might attack?*

21 What was the Pale?

By the end of the Middle Ages most of Ireland was controlled by great lords, either Irish or 'English by blood', who paid little attention to the king of England. Only a small area around Dublin known as the Pale still followed English fashions and laws and looked to the English king for support and leadership. How was the Pale different from the rest of Ireland? How was the rest of Ireland governed?

The Pale

In 1435 the Irish Parliament sent a report to England: 'The land of Ireland is well nigh destroyed and inhabited with enemies and rebels; so much so that out of the counties of Dublin, Meath, Louth and Kildare that join together there only remains an area scarcely thirty miles in length and twenty miles in breadth where men answer the king's writs and commandments.'

Parliament exaggerated, but the English government had lost control over many areas. The justiciar did not travel to distant areas; fewer parts of the country paid tax and only the four counties named in the report regularly sent representatives to Parliament.

In the fifteenth century the parts of these four counties closest to Dublin came to be known as 'the Pale'. A pale was a pole stuck in the ground as part of a fence. As time went by 'the Pale' came to mean the area within this imaginary fence, rather than the fence itself. At different times the Pale landowners built ditches around the area to stop Irish raiders stealing the cattle of the settlers. As time went by the inhabitants of the Pale came to see their part of Ireland as the last remaining foothold for English civilisation. They still used English law, spoke English, rode their horses in the English manner and sent their children to England to be educated. They regarded the Irish as their enemies, but they also distrusted the great English lords outside the Pale because they thought they were too gaelicised.

A Part of the Pale ditch and a map of the Pale

1 *How far is it from Dundalk to Saggart and Athboy to the coast?*

2 *Why did some towns have walls?*

3 *Would Gerald of Wales have been surprised by what this map shows?*

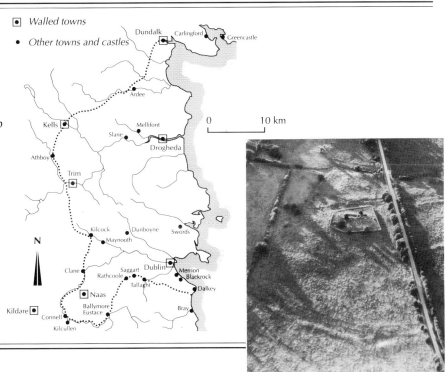

Walled towns
Other towns and castles

Dundalk · Carlingford · Greencastle
Ardee
Kells · Mellifont
Slane
Athboy · Drogheda
Trim
Kilcock · Dunboyne · Swords
Maynooth
Clane · Saggart · Dublin · Merrion · Blackrock
Rathcoole · Tallaght · Dalkey
Naas
Kildare · Ballymore Eustace · Bray
Connell
Kilcullen

0   10 km

N

The great lords

By the fifteenth century the kings of England were too poor to send large armies to Ireland so they allowed the most important English lords there to govern the country for them. Only they were strong enough to protect the Pale from the Irish. In the fifteenth century, three great families controlled Ireland in turn; the Butlers who were earls of Ormond, the Fitzgeralds who were earls of Desmond and their cousins the Fitzgeralds who were earls of Kildare.

To keep this control these earls had to have dealings with their Irish neighbours and to be ready to speak Irish and use Brehon law when it suited them. The English of the Pale objected to these close contacts. What they hated most was that the earls had taken up an Irish system of taxation and were trying to force this on the Pale. This system was called 'coign and livery'. It meant that an earl, instead of housing and feeding his own soldiers would make the tenants on his lands look after them.

The English of the Pale complained bitterly to the English kings about this custom and in 1463 Edward IV ordered the justiciar, who was then the Earl of Desmond, to stop 'that damnable and unlawful extortion and oppression called coign and livery'. The earls refused to become justiciars unless they were allowed to collect taxes as they saw fit. The English of the Pale might complain, but they were not willing or able to pay for their own security.

Poynings Law

At the end of the fifteenth century the eighth Earl of Kildare, Garret Mór, was in power. Ireland was much more settled than it had been since the Norman invasion, because he was powerful enough to control both the English and the Irish. But the king of England, Henry VII, was afraid he was too powerful. Garret Mór backed two attempts to remove Henry and replace him with another king. In 1494 Henry sent one of his supporters, Sir Edward Poynings, to Ireland to curb his independence.

Poynings set out to reduce the power of the Irish Parliament, which usually did as the Earl of Kildare ordered. He held a Parliament at Drogheda in 1494 which said that in future all laws passed in the English Parliament were automatically to apply in Ireland as well. Any laws passed by the Irish Parliament had first to be sent to England for the king's approval. This brought Ireland under tighter control. Kildare remained in power but his freedom of action was not as great as before. This was what the English of the Pale had wanted.

---

1 *Can you think of a common expression which involves 'the pale'. Do you see its origins in medieval Ireland?*

2 *How might life have been different for a peasant living on the lands of O Neill and one living on the lands of an earl of Desmond?*

22 The Normans in Ireland: Progress or decline?

This book has asked questions about the 'Norman era' in Irish history, when Ireland was dominated by a people who had conquered much of Europe. Was this a time of progress or did Ireland decline under the Normans?

1 Did the Normans ever control all of Ireland?

◉ *At the height of their power how much did they control? (see Units 7 and 13)*

What was the situation at the end of the Middle Ages? (see Unit 21)

Did the Normans bring peace to Ireland ? (see Units 7 and 14)

2 The Normans brought European models of law, government, agriculture and architecture to Ireland.

◉ *Did these change the parts of Ireland which they controlled? (see Units 8–12, 14, 16)*

Did they have an influence on the parts controlled by the Irish? (see Unit 15)

How far did Irish fashions influence the Normans? (see Unit 19)

3 The Normans said that they wanted to make the Church in Ireland more like the one in Europe and at first the Irish bishops supported them.

◉ *Did the Normans succeed in their aim for the Church? (see Units 11 and 16)*

4 Whether we think that the 'Norman era' was a time of progress or decline we can probably agree that the country was changed by their arrival in many basic ways. Their impact is still to be seen today. It is so powerful that we take it for granted. We can see it not only in old ruins but also in the language and law which are used in Ireland today, as well as the political problems we still face.

◉ *Look at the quotation from the declaration of the Irish Republic made by the first Dáil (Parliament) when it met in Dublin on 21 January 1919:*

'For 700 years the Irish people has never ceased to repudiate and has repeatedly protested in arms against foreign usurpation.'

i) *What was happening in Ireland 700 years before the Dáil declaration?*
ii) *'Usurpation' means taking political power which is not yours. Was the Norman conquest an example of foreign usurpation?*
iii) *'Repudiate' means refuse to accept. Did the Irish repudiate all Norman ways?*

5 Think about these points:

The declaration in 1919 was made in Irish and English.

In the Dáil there were people with surnames such as Plunkett, Cusack, FitzGerald and Burke. (See Unit 1)

The Dáil was a parliament. It met in Dublin.

Q *How can these facts be used to support the view that the Normans had a major impact on modern Irish politics?*

6 Some people today still try to decide who should be called Irish and who should not. This is not a new question. In the sixteenth century a Dubliner of Norman descent, Richard Stanihurst, lost patience with people who still distinguished between the two nations in Ireland; the Irish and the 'English by blood'. He insisted that he be called an Irishman, plain and simple, and added:

'He who dwells on the divisions among us shows that he is ashamed of his country. *But in my opinion* his country should rather be ashamed of him.'

Q *Do you agree?*